Budget Budgies Going, *Cheep*

Natasha Scholey

GWYDION

ISBN 978 0 9873894 6 6

Gwydion Books, PO Box 391, Stirling, SA, 5152, Australia

For
Jasmine
&
Ben

Wannabe Wallaby

Don't want to
be a wallaby,
Rather be a
roo,
All the
tourists
marvel,
Taking
pictures at
the zoo,
Of giant red
kangaroos,
Boxing with
one another,

Towering over me, I'm overlooked,
In favour of big brother,
I'm a wannabe roo,
Too small to get a mention,
Even when red lounges about,
He still gets all the attention.
I'd rather be a roo,
My face on postcards home,
I'm a wannabe roo,
Five feet I'd like to grow!

Busy Day

Lazily opens a single eye,
Watching the world pass busily by,
Stretches,
Slinks away,
Off to find a patch of shade,
To watch the world pass busily by.

When evening
draws near,
Pricks up his
ears,
Preens,
Stretches,
Yawns,
Slinks
purposely
away,

To find his dinner waiting there,
The human smiles and asks him,
What he's been up to today,
He answers with a stare,
That seems to suggest he's been busy,
Watching the world go by.

Little devil smile,
So sweet I want to pet you,
Deadly jaws snap closed.

Tra la la

I sing when I am merry,
I sing when I am blue,
How I wish my neighbours did,
Enjoy my singing too.

They close all their windows,
And begin to complain,
They shout abuse and tell me how
I will make it rain.

I know it should
not deter me,
I should not fill
with doubt,
But perhaps I
should refrain and
sing,
When next there
is a drought.

Leaves: A Lot To Be Desired

Oh leave me alone,
I'm eating my tea,
Yes it's a leaf all right,
It's yellow, can't you see?
No, it's not particularly palatable,
Provides no pleasure,
It's kind of chewy and bland,
Quite bitter to measure.
How I long for little fruits,
Or nuts and long sweet grass,
Yet, I am stuck with eating leaves,
On which I'd rather pass.

Shaggy Kangaroo

Shaggy macropod,
Herbivore, resting in shade,
Grazing marsupial

BBQ

Sizzling,
Popping,
Smells of cooking
meat,
Salivating in
expectation,
Of tonight's
barbecue feast.

Searing,
Bubbling,
Marinated meat
upon the bone,
Mouth watering in
anticipation,
Of tonight's
barbecue at home.

Galahs Galore

Pink parrot, scree scree,
Sociable, acrobatic,
Loud playful antics.

Rainbow

Dispersion of light,
Refraction of a raindrop,
Can't reach pot of gold.

My Furry Friend

Little possum,
Sweet are you,
Fluffy and furry,
If I catch you eating
my plants again,
Then you'd better
scurry.

Little possum,
Fur so soft,
Curly tail so cute,
But if you wake me
one more time,
I'll give you the
boot.

Budget Budgies

Wanna parrot?
Going *cheep,*
Good homes wanted,
Parrots in need,
We've every type of parrot,
To meet your means,
We've budgies on a budget!
Just keep their cages clean,
Make sure you feed them twice a day
And they'll repeat what you say.
Don't neglect them or misuse them,
Or budget budgies may,

Use some choice language,
You don't want kids to say.
Budgies on a budget,
All day they tweet and talk,
Much better than these larger birds,
All *they* do is squawk.

Fifty dollars
and they're
yours.
Love them,
don't mistreat
them,
Don't leave
them in the
lurch,
And it will be a
good long
while,
Before they
fall off their
perch!

Sunset

Glorious red,
Streaks across evening sky,
Intermingled with radiant orange.
Yellow of setting sun sinks out of sight,
A trail of blazing comet tails in its
wake.
If there is a god above,
Surely He must be a painter.

Where's Koali?

Guests have come to see the koalas,
Not so interested in me,
Heh, where's Koali?
Peering into Eucalypts,
A rustle peeks their interest,
No, just a lorikeet,
Heh, where's koali?
There are usually one or
two hanging about the garden,
Typical when guests come,
They seem to have gone,
Heh, where's Koali?
Perusing from the deck,
No koala in sight,

Into backyard bush,
Searching until fall of
night,
Heh, where's koali?
Guests come back inside,
Disgruntled with no
sighting,
Koala's decided to hide,
Heh, where's koali?
Guests have gone to bed,
I get ready too,
Outside my bedroom
door I see,
A koala doing a poo,
Oh, there's Koali!

Cockatoodleboodle

Cacophony of cockatoos,
Announcing and demanding,
Squabbles break out,
Courtship and dancing,
Squawking and competing,
Tearing up the joint,
Cacophony of cockatoos,
You bunch of feathered louts!

Blue Bee Or Not Blue Bee

Busy life-giver,
Amegilla Cingulata,
Habitat threatened.

A Sticky Situation

This is my stick,
Go and get your own,
I know you're only jealous,
That you can't take it home,
It's great for making music on,
Well in my imagination,
Or I can chew it like this,
It gets me some attention,
It's my stick and I won't let it go,

I'm sure *you* can find one too,
I like to wave it in the air,
And fend off kangaroos,
It's my stick, my very own.
I know it's rather bit,
But it's of sentimental value,
That's my story and I'm *sticking* to it!

DUCK!

DUCK!
Someone shouts,
So I do,
I never know if they're seeing me,
Or saying what to do,
Once I did assume,
They were greeting me,
So I didn't duck in time,
And hit a fallen tree.

I Spy Sea Spray

I spy sea spray,
By the seashore,
Six feet sideways and seven feet tall,
Sea spray like shattered glass,
Seven hundred and seventy-six shards of
sapphire,
Seven thousand seven hundred and seventy-six
sequins of salt,
Seventy seven thousand seven hundred and
sixty spatters of sparkle.

I spy sea spray,
by the seashore,
Saturates sands,
Spluttering over shells,
Shiny seaweed soaked and splayed,
Shouting salutations over sable stones,
Sunburned sunbathers', salubrious salvation,
Scattering sea saliva to sailors' satisfaction,
Slipping over sandals,
Scintillating senses,
Shrinking back to scenic splendour.
I spy sea spray by the seashore.

Gullible Gull

I'm a gullible gull,
I believe what everyone says,
A fish convinced me to put him back in the
sea,
Just the other day,
I'm a gullible gull,
I believe what everyone tells me,
I always take them at their word
And buy any rubbish they sell me.

Sealed With A Kiss

Two amphibious mammals,
Two peas in our pod,
Just snogging on the foreshore,
Locomoting ourselves through water,
With a flip of our flippers,
Return to beach to smooch some more.
"Woah, fish breath!!"
"Well, it's a good job I'm phocine, not otarid,
Or else hearing your hurtful sentiment
might make me blubber!"

Dingoes Playing Bingo

When the sun goes down,
Animals come out to play,
Up to all sorts of antics,
You don't see in the day.
Dingoes playing bingo!
Hawks who like to talk,
Crickets playing cricket,
Storks who like to stalk,
Skates who like to skate,
Sharks who like to bark,
Meerkats versus pandas,
Playing football in the park.

Sheep who like to beep,
Rabbits who can row,
Penguins race on pogo sticks,
With many miles to go.
Tortoise likes to make some noise,
Snakes they like to bake,
Servals sing all night long,
Until their voices ache.

Wombats like to bat,
Whilst voles prefer to bowl,
Both black bears and great grizzly bears,
Stare into a hole.
Bees like to break-dance,
Fleas like to flee,
When hogs decide to jog,
In circles round a tree.
Pikes they like to hike,
Drongos like to dance,
Jaguars they can juggle,
And fight with sword and lance.

Ravens they can rollerblade,
Whilst foxes they do fiddle,
Chipmunks like to play charades,
And chipmunks in the middle.
Horses playing hockey,
Newts prefer netball,
Piranhas good at water polo,
In the swimming pool.
Hedgehogs they like high jump,
Bettong sits on bum,
Camels form a choir,
And sing 'til day is come.

www.ingramcontent.com/pod-product-compliance
Lightning Source LLC
LaVergne TN
LVHW010033070426
835508LV00005B/307